Life As a
Frog

Victoria Parker

Raintree

Chicago, Illinois

© 2004 Raintree
Published by Raintree, a division of Reed Elsevier, Inc.
Chicago, Illinois
Customer Service 888-363-4266
Visit our website at www.raintreelibrary.com

For information, address the publisher:
Raintree, 100 N. LaSalle, Suite 1200, Chicago, IL 60602

Printed and bound in China by South China Printing Company.
12 11 10 09
10 9 8 7 6 5 4

Library of Congress Cataloging-in-Publication Data:
Parker, Victoria.
  Life as a frog / Victoria Parker.
     p. cm. -- (Life as)
Includes bibliographical references and index.
Summary: Takes a comprehensive look at the life cycle of the frog.
  ISBN 1-4109-0627-2 (Library Binding-hardcover) -- ISBN 1-4109-0653-1 (Paperback)

  ISBN 978-1-4109-0627-4 (Library Binding-hardcover) -- ISBN 978-1-4109-0653-3 (Paperback)

  1. Frogs--Life cycles--Juvenile literature. [1. Frogs.] I. Title.
II. Series: Parker, Victoria. Life as.
  QL668.E2P298 2004
  597.8--dc21
                              2003008281

Acknowledgments
The publishers would like to thank the following for permission to reproduce photographs: p. 15 Andy Purcell; pp. 4-5
Bruce Coleman (Jane Burton); pp. 22-23 (Feliz Labhardt); p. 6 FLPA (© W Meinderts) Foto Natur; p. 7 Heather Angel;
pp. 8, 9 NHPA (© G I Bernard); pp. 10-11, 12, 14 (Stephen Dalton); p. 16-17 Oxford Scientific Films; p. 13 OSF (©
Paul Franklin); p. 20-21 OSF (Ian West); p. 18-19 Woodfall Wild Images

Cover photograph reproduced with permission of Naturepl.com/William Osborn

Some words are shown in bold, **like this.** You can find out
what they mean by looking in the glossary on page 24.

Contents

Frog Eggs

Look into a pond. You might see a blob of jelly with black dots.

Hatching

The eggs **hatch.**

Out come tiny tadpoles.

tail

Tadpoles have long tails.
Their tails help them swim to find food.

Growing

In a few weeks, a tadpole begins to grow legs.

The tadpole's legs grow longer.
Its tail gets shorter.

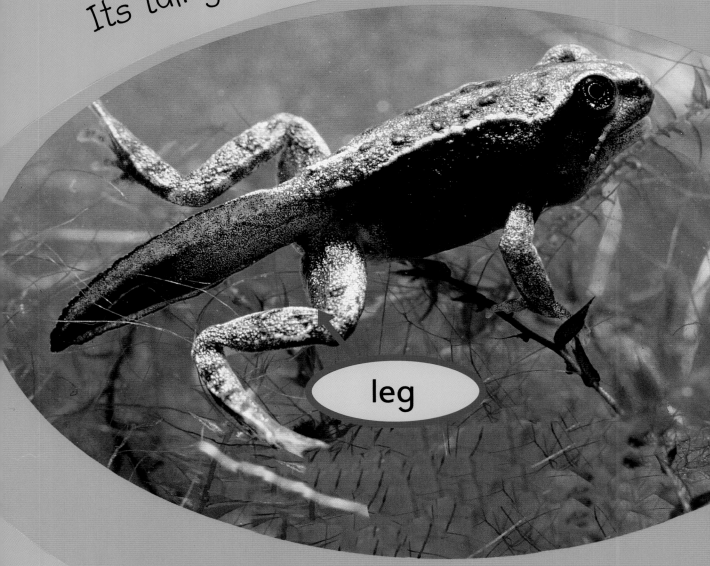

leg

Changing

The tadpole changes into a frog.

The frog has four legs.

A Frog's Life

Frogs live in ponds and rivers.

They spend most of their time in the water.

webbed
foot

Frogs use their webbed
feet to help them swim.

Life on Land

Frogs spend some time on land.
They hop on their long, strong legs.

Frogs hide in damp, dark places.

Eating

Frogs eat bugs. They catch worms with their sticky tongues.

Mating

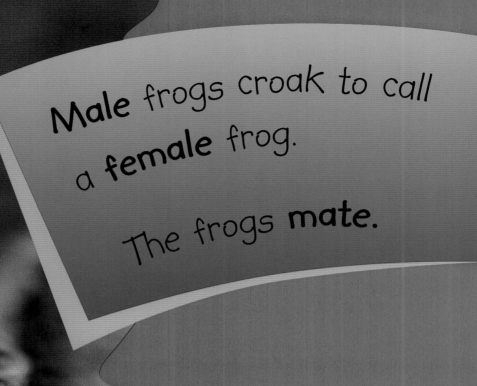

Male frogs croak to call a **female** frog.

The frogs **mate**.

Laying Eggs

The **female** frog lays **spawn** in the pond.

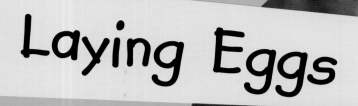

Inside the spawn, new tadpoles are ready to **hatch**.

New Frog Quiz

How did these frogs get into the pond?

Look for the answer on page 24!

Glossary

female   girl frog

hatch   to come out of an egg

male   boy frog

mate   when two living things come together to make babies

spawn   jelly-like blobs that are frogs' eggs

Frog Life Cycle

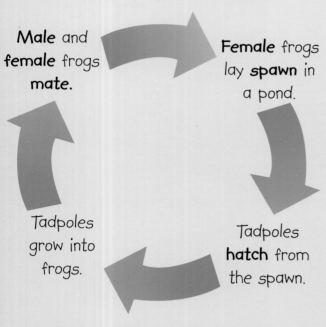

Male and **female** frogs **mate.**

Female frogs lay **spawn** in a pond.

Tadpoles **hatch** from the spawn.

Tadpoles grow into frogs.

This is how new frogs got into the pond on pages 22 and 23.

Index